DESERTS

Alexis Roumanis

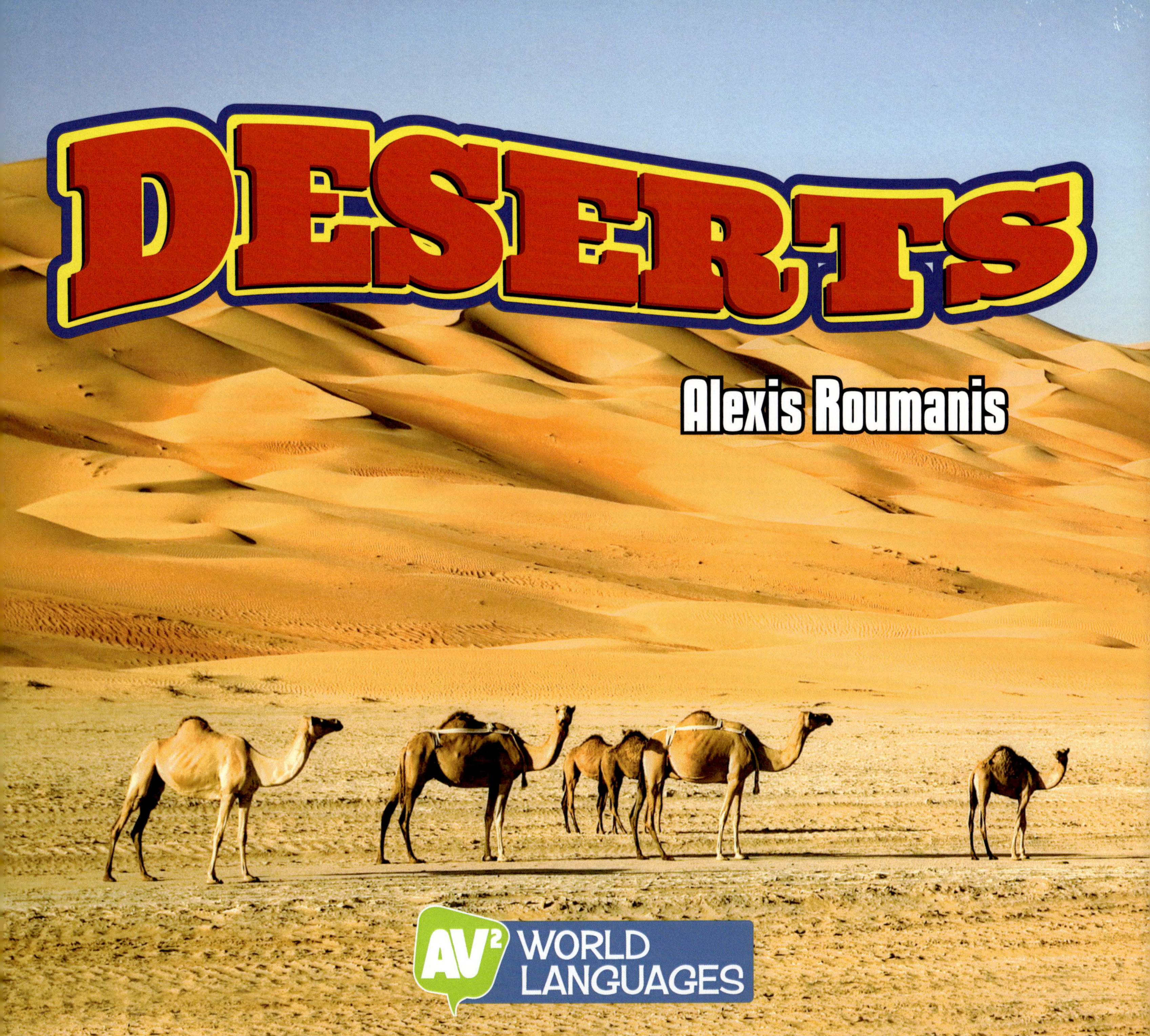

AV² WORLD LANGUAGES

AV² WORLD LANGUAGES

Go to **av2books.com**, and enter this book's unique code.

BOOK CODE

AVE84848

Easily move through highly visual pages.

Toggle between your **eight books** in **eight languages.**

Published by AV² by Weigl
350 5th Avenue, 59th Floor New York, NY 10118
Website: www.av2books.com

Library of Congress Control Number: 2018948268

ISBN 978-1-4896-6921-6 (hardcover)
ISBN 978-1-4896-6922-3 (multi-user eBook)

Printed in the United States of America in Brainerd, Minnesota
1 2 3 4 5 6 7 8 9 0 22 21 20 19 18

072018
012518

Project Coordinator: Jared Siemens
Designer: Mandy Christiansen

Weigl acknowledges iStock and Getty Images as the primary image suppliers for this title.

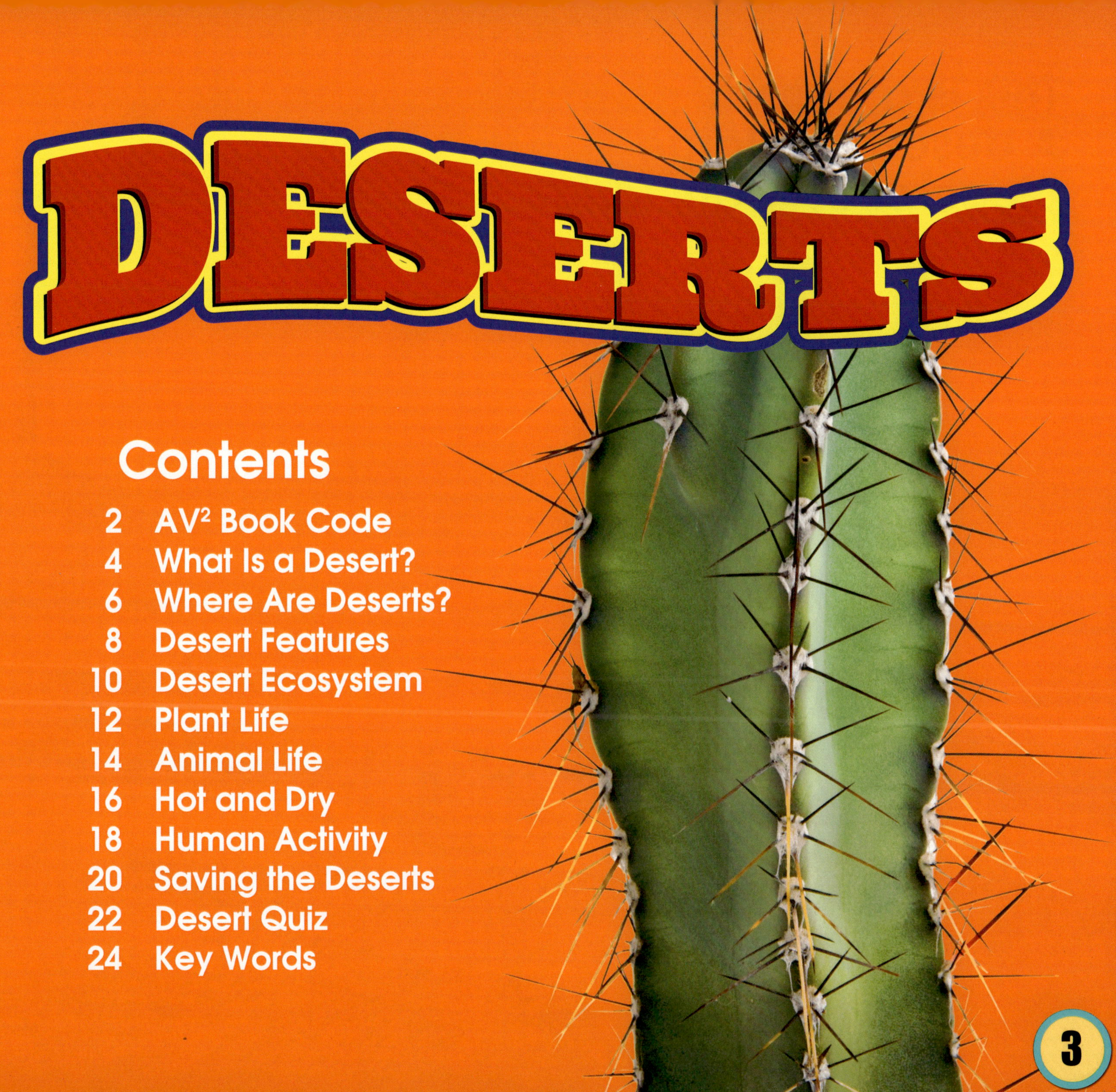

DESERTS

Contents

This is a desert.
A desert is a large
piece of very dry land.

Most deserts are found near Earth's equator. Deserts are almost always very hot or very cold.

The biggest hot desert in the world is the Sahara Desert.

Some deserts have many large piles of sand called dunes.

Other deserts have large rocks or fields of ice and snow.

The regal horned lizard needs heat from the Sun to warm its body.

Gila woodpeckers often make their homes in Saguaro cacti.

The Namib Desert beetle gathers water from morning fog to drink.

A desert ecosystem is a place made up of animals and plants that need each other in order to live.

Bull snakes often live in holes made by other animals.

The lesser long-nosed bat eats nectar from cactus flowers.

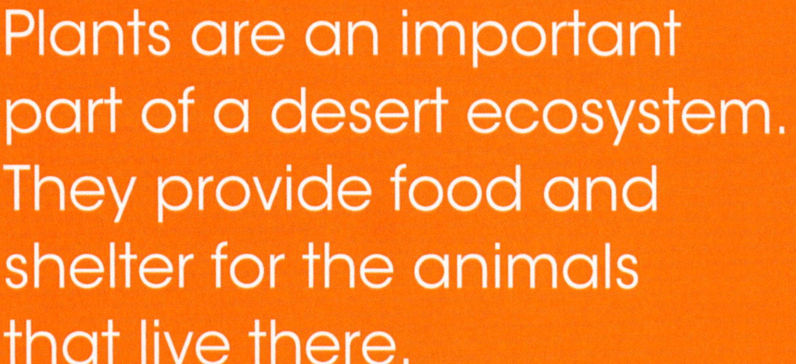

Plants are an important part of a desert ecosystem. They provide food and shelter for the animals that live there.

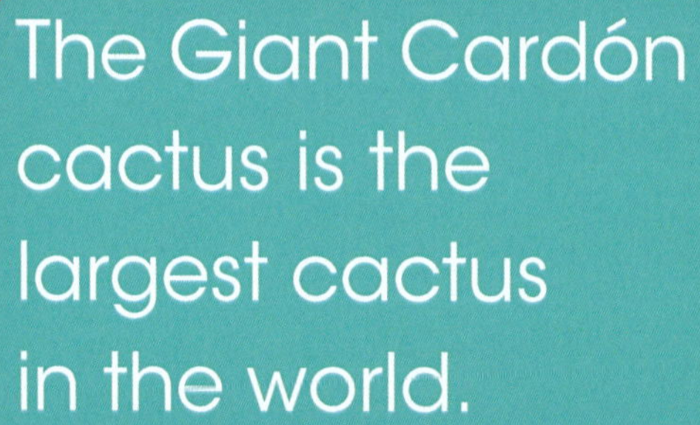

The Giant Cardón cactus is the largest cactus in the world.

Tumbleweeds use the wind to help spread their seeds around.

The saguaro cactus can hold 201 gallons (761 liters) of water.

Joshua trees need the yucca moth to help them make seeds.

The California fan palm can live up to 90 years.

Camels can live in the desert for about seven days without drinking water.
Desert tortoises dig holes to trap rainwater for drinking.

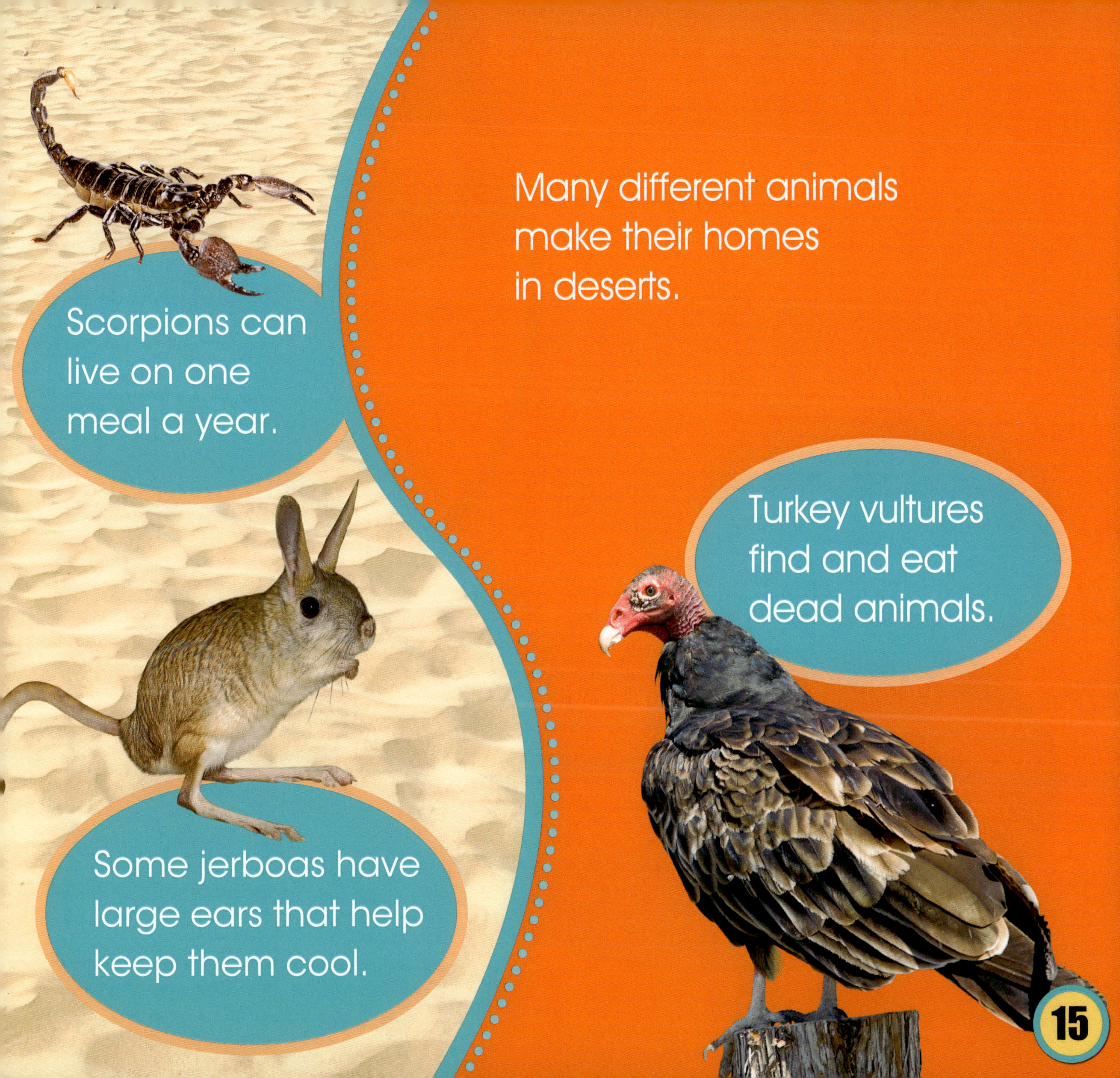
Scorpions can live on one meal a year.
Many different animals make their homes in deserts.
Turkey vultures find and eat dead animals.
Some jerboas have large ears that help keep them cool.

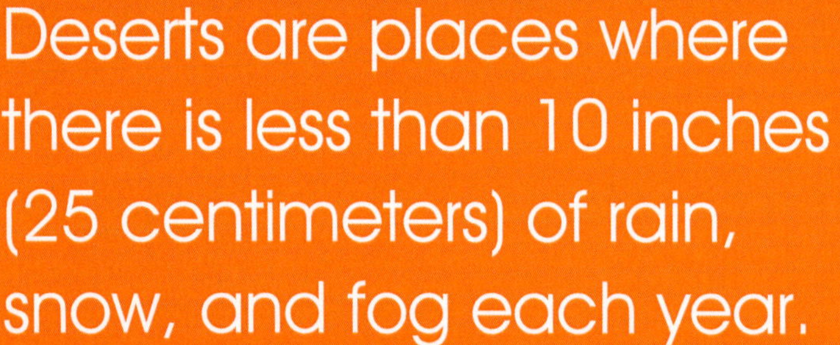

Deserts are places where there is less than 10 inches (25 centimeters) of rain, snow, and fog each year.

Earth's hottest temperature of 134 degrees Fahrenheit (56.7 degrees Celsius) was recorded in Death Valley, California.

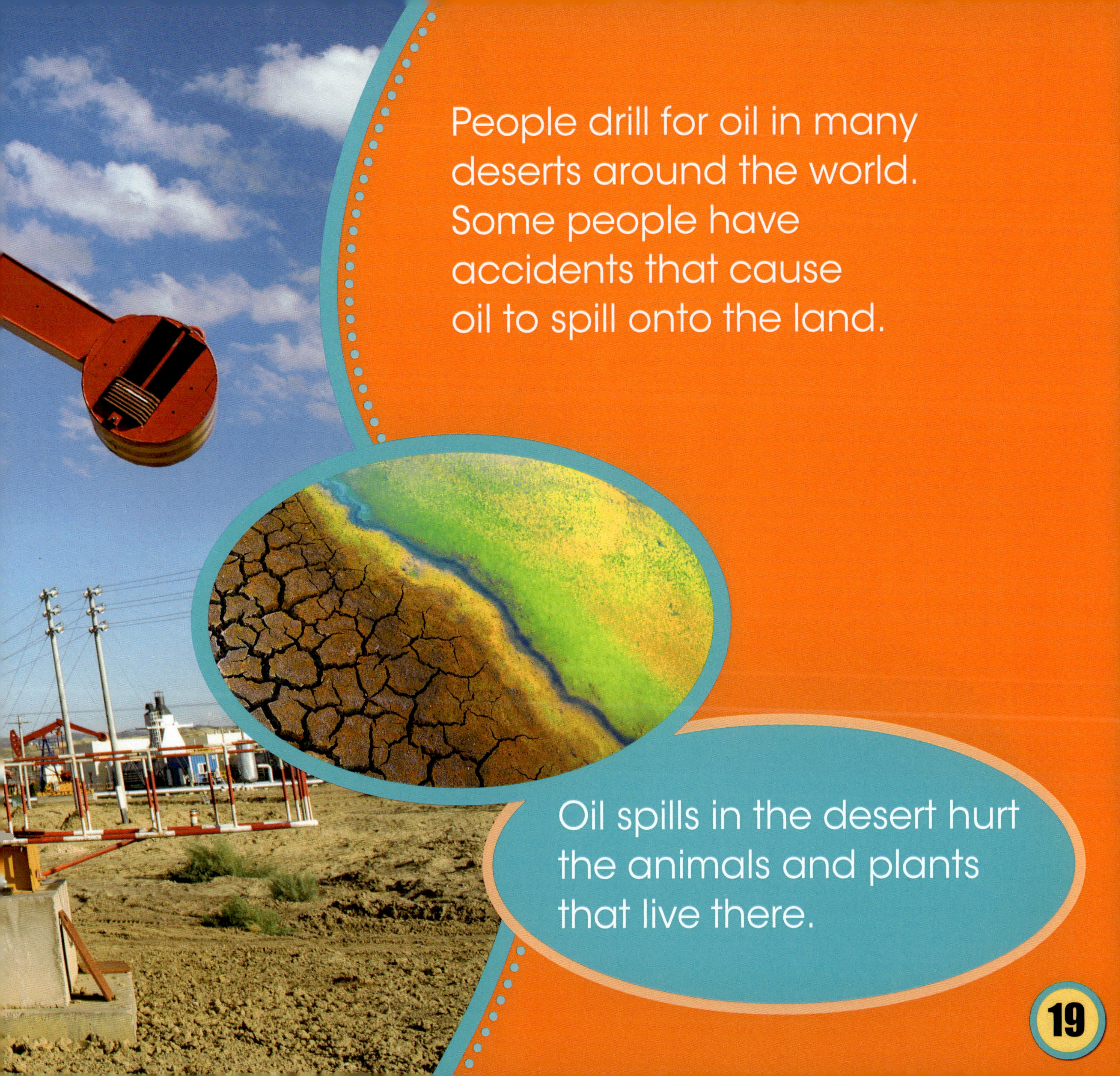

People drill for oil in many deserts around the world. Some people have accidents that cause oil to spill onto the land.

Oil spills in the desert hurt the animals and plants that live there.

Some people like to drive off-road in the desert. Driving off-road can harm animals and plants.

People should stay on the roads and trails to keep animals and plants safe.

YAMAHA
PERU
ARGENTINA
CHILE
281
SIX2
YAMAHA
elf
ÖHLINS
CARIGNANI
BLACKFORESTPOWERSPORTS.com
FRANCE
EQUIPEMENT
RK

Desert Quiz

See what you have learned about desert ecosystems.

Find these desert animals and plants in the book. What are their names?

KEY WORDS

Research has shown that as much as 65 percent of all written material published in English is made up of 300 words. These 300 words cannot be taught using pictures or learned by sounding them out. They must be recognized by sight. This book contains 72 common sight words to help young readers improve their reading fluency and comprehension. This book also teaches young readers several important content words, such as proper nouns. These words are paired with pictures to aid in learning and improve understanding.

Page	Sight Words First Appearance
4	a, is, land, large, of, this, very
7	almost, always, are, Earth, found, in, most, near, or, the, world
8	and, have, many, other, some
10	from, homes, its, make, needs, often, their, to, water
11	animals, by, each, eats, live, long, made, place, plants, that, up
12	an, around, food, for, help, important, part, there, they, use
13	can, them, trees, years
14	about, days, without
15	different, find, keep, on, one
16	than, was, where
19	people
20	like, off, should

Page	Content Words First Appearance
4	desert, piece
7	equator, Sahara Desert
8	dunes, fields, ice, piles, rocks, sand, snow
10	beetle, body, cacti, fog, heat, lizard, Sun, woodpeckers
11	bat, ecosystem, flowers, holes, nectar, snakes
12	seeds, shelter, tumbleweeds, wind
13	palm, moth
14	camels, rainwater, tortoises
15	ears, jerboas, meal, scorpions, vultures
16	California, Death Valley, rain, temperature
19	accidents, oil
20	roads, trails